Contents

About The Author	2
About This Book	3
Introduction	5
Chapter 1: Current Trends	11
Chapter 2: The Psychology Of Choice and FREE	14
Chapter 3: 10 Core Elements Of An Effective Landing Page	20
Chapter 4: The Four-Step Lead Generation Process	47
Chapter 5: Life After The Landing Page	50
Chapter 6: Promoting Your Landing Page	54
Chapter 7: Tools to Help You Create The Perfect Landing Page	59
Bonus Offers	62
Thanks, And Good Luck!	63

About The Author

Darren Hignett has more than 20 years of experience, working in marketing roles ranging from being a Product Manager for global businesses, launching products globally to running his own marketing agency, supporting other businesses to make their marketing more effective.

His passion for marketing started with a degree in International Business - a 4 year course with a very strong focus on marketing theory with concepts such as how to define your target market, how to understand their needs and how to create the right message and benefits in a way that customers understand and will want to buy from you.

This book shares his knowledge and expertise in designing websites that generate leads and sales including his proven 4 step lead generation process.

About This Book

Note: This book has been updated to reflect trends for 2020 and beyond! It now includes updated tips and an updated list of apps that you can use!

If you want to convert more website visitors into customers, then this book is for you. Every year, vast amounts of time and money are wasted on underperforming websites that don't generate business as they should and many companies are unaware that they could convert 10 or even 20 times more visitors into paying customers – and with less effort than they do currently!

In this book, I will highlight how many websites today might be professionally built and look good but are not optimized to convert site visitors into paying customers. By looking at how websites are structured in terms of content, layout, wording and even the colors used we can generate more sales from a website and in many cases with less design effort.

A particular focus in this book is on what's commonly referred to as landing pages but many of the elements discussed around the content of a page can easily be applied to larger more complex websites such as eCommerce stores.

Having just a simple single landing page that's well designed could make a huge difference to your sales and marketing activity. This book guides you through the process and design of a landing page, highlighting the critical elements required to convert site visitors into paying customers.

We will also cover:

- The importance of power words that prompt visitors to take action
- How the psychology of color on your site affects what action visitors take
- How to use a call to action to capture lead information and what you should do after capturing visitor details to convert their visit into a sale

The book also includes over 50 apps that you can use to create the perfect landing page that converts!

Note: There are also special offers including lots of free stuff throughout this book. Don't forget to check out some great offers at the back of the book when you have finished reading!

Introduction

Businesses spend millions (if not billions worldwide) every year on websites with the aim of winning over customers but the number of visitors to these sites don't stay on the site for very long, don't become paying customers in the long term and without doubt a lot of that money is wasted on the design and support of these sites.

Think about any website creation you have been involved in the design or creation of or the last website you visited with an intention to buy something. If the site was professionally done it most likely contained lots of attractive pages with images, well-written headlines and lots of pages with links to them to give you the feeling that the company is professional and has lots of information to offer.

We can arguably suggest that this is good. After all, a site with very little information and poor or no images gives a feeling of emptiness and doubt about the credibility of the business. A showcase website that looks amazing must be the answer, right?

It all sounds great. But now consider these astonishing facts:

- The average visitor stays on a website for less than 30 seconds!
- Typically, less than 50% of visitors navigate to a second page or even scroll down the page!
- Only 2-5% of website visits convert into orders and for many businesses, it's much less!

Having a well-designed website looks professional and gives a good feeling to any visitors that might be considering buying from you. That's understandable. But, what if you could increase your conversion rate with less effort? What if you don't need all those pages and just a few well-designed pages could double or triple your sales?

Imagine this scenario:

You have 200 visitors a month to your site and have a conversion rate of 2% (so 4 out of every 200 visitors become customers). If you have an average order value of £100 (or dollars) then £400 a month is generated from your website each month (4 customers x £100).

You could invest in marketing to increase the number of visitors to your site. But, while this will work and should be used as part of a marketing plan, it does increase marketing cost if you are using methods such as pay per click advertising and sometimes, as the visitor numbers increase, the conversion rate can drop slightly as the quality of visitors drops.

Alternatively, you could work on better ways to convert website visitors. Just by increasing the conversion rate from 2% to 4% means a doubling of sales from £400 to £800 a month. And that's without increasing the number of visitors to your site!

Increasing the conversion rate on a website shouldn't require a complete overhaul of the site. The creation of a single landing page, for example, will make a big difference and require a lot less effort.

In this book, we will go through the current trends and customer habits that need to be considered when developing a landing page. We will then cover the critical elements needed in a landing page that increase the chances of conversion.

First, let's cover a couple of quick questions about landing pages:

What is a landing page?

A page you want customers to 'land on'. Or put another way, it's the first page you want visitors to see that is targeted to what they are looking for. A landing page could be used as part of a marketing campaign offering a free gift such as an eBook or a physical item delivered by post (think of calendars, diaries or sample product to trial). It could also be product-specific with a focus on the visitor making an inquiry or clicking the buy button.

A business doesn't need to be restricted to one landing page. You may have several landing pages for different products or offers with each landing page containing content that is tailored to the solution or campaign.

A personal fitness trainer, for example, may use 2 landing pages. The first one to target people who want to focus on losing weight and the target audience for this landing page is people who might not take exercise regularly or who want to cut back on the amount of food (especially unhealthy food!) that they consume. The second landing page may be focussed on customers who want to reach a much higher level of fitness. They may be training for a long-distance run or want to build up their muscle mass for sporting activities.

Whereas the weight loss landing page might have content around calorie counting and the benefits of weight loss, the landing page focused on increasing fitness might be more 'hardcore' with exercise and diet information for building up strength or body muscle. The images, content including wording and call to action would need to be distinctively different on each of those landing pages. People wanting to lose weight, for example, would not be interested in a free guide to building up their abs or how to get a six-pack!

Why can't I just use the home page?

The homepage is too generic and not effective for targeted marketing campaigns. If you sell various products, it's more effective if you direct visitors directly to a page with an offer or with information on the products that are relevant to them. When a visitor lands on the home page, he or she will most likely have to navigate through a page of text, images, and videos just to find the product or service they want.

The more a visitor has to click through various pages to find what he or she wants, the greater the chance there is of losing them.

There are times when it's best to quote your home page, such as in email signatures and business cards, but for marketing campaigns, a specific landing page is a lot more effective.

A recruitment campaign should direct job seekers to specific recruitment pages rather than have them land on the home page and then wonder where to find the information they were expecting. A workshop or seminar campaign should direct people wanting to attend the event to a specific page with more relevant information on the event and easy access to reserving their place at the event.

The landing page should make it as easy and simple as possible for the target audience to find what they want and take action. The content on the page should also be more relevant, highlighting the benefits of what they are interested in. The home page, in many cases, just doesn't do that.

Terminology time!

Before we go into landing page design and trends, let's briefly cover a few terms that you will come across. Although the wording in this book has been kept as simple as possible, avoiding technical terms and jargon, the following terms are important to know!

Bounce Rate:

This is the number of visitors who only visit one page on your site. If 60 out of every 100 visitors only visit one page and leave your site before either closing down the web browser or going to another site then the bounce rate is 60%. Usually the lower the figure the better!

CTA or Call to action:

A call to action is, as the name suggests, a call or message to prompt someone to take action - and while this sounds straightforward, many marketers either fail to have the right call to action, position it badly or don't have a call to action at all in their marketing!

The call to action (or CTA) can vary depending on various factors such as the type of campaign, the channel being used and how ready a customer is to buy. In printed marketing and on a website the CTA could be a special offer and with a face-to-face meeting or phone call with a potential customer, the CTA could be to arrange the next meeting or to email more information.

Take it steady, or get to the point?

For most businesses, there are always customers who are ready to buy and customers who want to find out more about your brand, what you offer and if you are a trusted brand to buy from. Both types of customers should be targeted with different marketing campaigns. The customer who is willing to buy is more likely to accept a call to action that's direct, such as 'if you order today then you will receive an extra month for free and 20% off' but a customer who is still in the early stages of making a decision is more likely to need a softer approach as part of a longer sales. In this case, offering a call to action such as a free guide on how to achieve something or another offer that isn't immediately going to get the sale is more effective.

Here are some ways you can be more effective in your marketing, not just on your landing page:

Positioning

A CTA needs to be easily accessible and having a CTA at the top and the bottom of marketing materials and landing pages is more effective. If your website has lots of images and words then the call to action needs to stand out and having it visible at the top makes it easier to find.

Have a CTA!

It sounds obvious but it's easy to forget a call to action. Check your marketing and communications to make sure you have a call to action as much as sensibly possible. This should include web pages, marketing materials, blog posts, and your email signature - even if it's just a link to drive someone to read your blog posts.

Make it desirable, even irresistible!

Sorry but 'click here', 'sign up' and 'submit' don't get me excited and want to take action. Signing up and submitting are also considered negative subconsciously (are you ready to submit or commit to 'signing up' even if it's just for a regular email newsletter?). Phrases such as 'save me money', 'show me how' and 'join' are more powerful and more likely to prompt a potential customer to take action. We will talk about this in more detail later on.

Chapter 1: Current Trends

Before covering the key elements of a landing page, it's important to understand the current trends in technology and marketing as well as customer trends. Technology is moving fast and this is hugely impacting the way we browse and make purchases.

Here are some trends that affect customer behaviors and influence the critical elements of an effective landing page:

Going Mobile: More people now browse the web on mobile phones and tablets than on a desktop and landing pages need to be designed to be easy to navigate on small screens. If a visitor goes to your site on their mobile phone and can't read what the site says or can't navigate it, then they are very unlikely to take any positive action such as making an inquiry or a purchase.

The critical message and wording on any landing page must be positioned so that it stands out on small mobile screens. It needs to be clearly visible along with any form that is used for capturing visitor details. The form also needs to be easy for visitors to fill in (small screens and pop up keyboards on the screen are not always the easiest to use when you have lots to read or data to fill in!).

Busy Lives: The pressures of everyday life mean people have less time available. A report in 2016 found that we now have a shorter attention span than a goldfish and the consequences of this are that if we don't find what we want immediately or it's too much effort then we quickly lose interest. Grabbing someone's attention as quickly as possible when marketing is essential.

You may offer lots of great information on your website but fewer people are now reading this content. It doesn't mean your content isn't useful or isn't' interesting. It's most likely that the visitor to your site is short on time or has been easily distracted by the phone or doorbell ringing, the Facebook notification on their desktop or something else that causes intrigue!

If you want a visitor to understand the benefits of what you are offering and take action it needs to be as clear as possible and as quickly as possible. Making the visitor read lots of content before taking action will reduce the chances of your web page being a success.

The internet is 'overcrowded': The barriers to getting online for businesses are very low leading to a huge growth in the number of online businesses - and they are all vying for the attention of the customer. It's the era of information overload as customers are bombarded with information to lure them to buy and this is compounded by the fact we all lead busy lives. Having a message or offer that's compelling is important if a business is to stand out from the crowd.

We will refer to these trends throughout the book with examples of how a well-designed landing page should be created to fit the trends of the future and overcome issues such as customers leading busy lives!

Over the years, the human mind has developed and adapted to its surroundings and the trends above are heavily impacting the way we make purchases. Take the growth of Amazon for example. There are many reasons for the success of Amazon and one of those, is the way it has responded to the trends mentioned above.

With the thousands of new eCommerce businesses that set up every day, which ones should you trust? And do you have time to research the web endlessly to find the right product from the right company at the right price? Many people simply opt to buy from Amazon.

By being a single portal for all products and solutions, their offer is compelling in an overcrowded market. People lead busy lives and want to order quickly and easily from a trusted source and they have taken this to new levels with one-click ordering and new technology such as Amazon Echo and their DASH solutions (which are wireless buttons allowing you to order more washing powder-or pet food with the click of a button). Both of these are great solutions for people with busy lives and are, at the moment, unique compared to what the competition offers although Google is challenging the dominance of Amazon Echo with its own solution.

The smart move to sell Kindle Fire tablets which are geared around the shopping experience on Amazon has also kept them up to date with the trend of going mobile.

Amazon is an extreme example that includes more than just a great landing page but it highlights how focusing on the trends of the future and providing customers with what they want online is important and this should be considered when creating your landing page. Even in its early days, Amazon was not known for having a pretty, flash looking website yet its ability to convert visitors into paying customers was core to its success.

The Amazon website may not have been pretty (and probably still isn't the most beautiful site to browse?) but it had the right images, headlines and call to actions in the right place. These elements are as important in an eCommerce site as they are in a highly effective landing page.

Chapter 2: The Psychology Of Choice and FREE

Before we go through the critical elements of an effective landing page (chapter 3), there are two elements of human behavior I would like to discuss. At this point, you may be thinking 'oh no, psychology doesn't interest me' or 'this must be the boring chapter, I'll just skip it' but bear with me. Understanding how you can use these two elements on your landing page could hugely impact your results. It will also help understand why the elements covered in chapter 3 are important.

The first element is **'choice'**. This is effectively the number of options that you give to a customer. Over the years, we have got used to an increasing range of options from different car brands and car types to places to shop for everyday consumables such as mobiles, stationery or home and kitchenware. You only have to walk down the aisle of your local supermarket to see how many kinds of cereal, sauces or wines and beers are available.

We have been programmed over the years to believe that a range of choice is good. Why settle for a small compact car in a green tint that you don't like when you can have a spacious SUV in the shiny silver or metallic black that you do you like - and with optional extras you love? Ask any consumer if they would like as much choice as possible and the answer will pretty much always be YES.

Unfortunately, too much choice for your customers can harm sales. Consider this:

In 2010, the Economist magazine[1] reported on research where jams were available to taste as samples outside a store and a coupon was offered to consumers to redeem on a jam they liked and could purchase in the store. When a choice of 24 jams was offered, 3% of consumers made a purchase but when the number of samples was reduced to only 6 options, the conversion rate (or the number of people who went on to make a purchase) increased from 3% to an incredible 30%. It seems like less choice made the decision to purchase much

---

[1] Source: http://www.economist.com/node/17723028

easier. Having too many choices meant that many consumers were overwhelmed by the choice and took an option that wasn't on the table - the decision to not make a purchase.

This inability to decide what to purchase is usually because as humans we like to take the easy choice. If none of the options is overwhelmingly desirable (ie. an option that beyond doubt is the one we want) then we will take the easy option which is to not commit to purchasing or even decide to do something that involves less commitment than parting with money (consider a website visitor is close to purchasing on your site and instead decides to read your blog articles or check out your social media profile instead of tapping the 'buy' button!).

This research in the Economist has been backed up over the years by various articles such as *Why Too Much Choice Is Stressing Us Out by the Guardian*[2] and books such as *The Paradox of Choice: Why More Is Less* by Barry Schwartz. It seems that although we like the idea of choice, it's not always a good thing. So what has this got to do with landing pages? Or Marketing in general?

When designing a landing page, it's important to have a single clear objective. If the page is offering a free eBook or white paper then you want the visitor to enter their email address and hit the button to receive their copy. If the page objective is to make a purchase, the objective is to drive the visitor towards clicking on the buy button. Offering a choice of options reduces the likelihood the visitor will take the action you want. Previously I mentioned that we lead busy lives and have shorter attention spans. Providing more options not only makes it harder for the visitor to decide what to do, it's also more likely to distract them from that very reason they arrived on the landing page in the first place.

Unwanted options might include offering 2 eBooks or distractions such as links to your social media profiles, blog page or About Us page. We will go through this in more detail in chapter 3 but it's important to understand that more options, as Barry Schwartz might say, is fewer sales.

---

[2] Source: https://www.theguardian.com/lifeandstyle/2015/oct/21/choice-stressing-us-out-dating-partners-monopolies

Let's put this into a possible business numbers scenario. If 30 people take action on your landing page every day, you want 100% of them (all 30) to click on the purchase button that generates that £20 sale. That equates to sales of £600 a day.

Now assume that you add a second choice or link to take a visitor elsewhere and that as a result, only 80% take the action you want (10% take no action as they can't decide and another 10% click on that new link you have offered instead).

Now we have only 27 people on average taking action every day instead of 30 (3 people can't decide or decide not to click on either of the links). Out of the 27 who take action, only 24 or 25 people are making a purchase - as 10% of the visitors decide to click on the second link that's been added. One small added option to a landing page has made a big difference to the conversion rate and sales generated on a daily basis. Over a 365 day year, that's £1,825 fewer sales!

This also has an impact on the wider area of marketing such as the number of products your business offers or the number of pricing options available. We won't go through these in this book but operating on the mantra of 'keep it simple' should be a must for any modern marketer!

And How About the Theory Of Free?

In his book, *Predictably Irrational*, Dan Ariely demonstrates how consumers are enticed so heavily by something free that it leads to decisions that might be worse off for them! The 0% interest on a credit card for the first 3 months followed by a much higher rate over the long term might be a worse decision for a consumer to take compared to an option from another bank offering a lower rate with no special introductory offer, but the idea of 0 or interest being 'free' gets the sale.

I should point out that I'm not endorsing the idea of luring customers to make purchases that make them worse off, or that you should start giving away your core products for free (after all the purpose of a business is to make money!) but using FREE as a marketing tool on your landing page and as part of a marketing campaign can be a highly effective way to succeed in marketing. If people are so allured by the idea of free that they take up offers that make them worse off, imagine how well it works when you offer something for free that adds value and benefits them!

So, why does FREE work?

According to Seth Godin in his marketing workshop, a customer's heart rate increases just before making their first purchase from a business. This reflects the risk involved for the customer - parting with money, the risks of buying from an unknown or proven source and the risks of the item being faulty. It may only be a small risk such as parting with a few pounds or dollars but the risk is enough to put a potential customer off purchasing.

According to Seth, offering an item for free removes those risks and the consequent increase in heart rate. If the first 'purchase' is free such as a trial or 'how to' guide then you are more likely to build trust with the customer and making a second purchase involving spending money is easier - and more likely to happen!

Talk about increasing heart rates and risks of purchasing might sound a bit profound but the takeaway is simple: if you offer something for free you are more likely to get the sale for the products or services your business makes money on.

Your landing page doesn't have to be focused on generating an immediate sale with a cash cost to the customer. In chapter 4, I talk about the proven 4 step lead generation process which includes a landing page and a lead generation product. You will see in chapter 4 how offering a free resource on a landing page can be a great way to generate good leads that you can convert into sales consistently over the long term.

One last final comment on the term 'free' as there are 2 different types of free products you can offer. In my book, *How To Create A Successful Email Marketing Campaign* (available on Amazon), I talk about 4 different types of products that every business should offer. These are the **Gift Product, Lead Generation Product, Core Product, and Upsell Product**.

Both the Gift and Lead Generation Products are used to generate sales of the Core Product and as such are both free - but the type of free they offer is not quite the same. Whereas the Gift Product is completely free with no commitment required from a customer (such as video tips publicly available on a YouTube channel) the Lead Generation Product requires a commitment that, arguably, is not completely free. The Lead Generation Product can be a free trial of your software or services but may require the customer to provide you with information such as their contact details or credit card details (for payment of continued services after the trial ends). There is 'completely free', and then there is 'free but with a commitment' - by the customer to provide something such as personal information which might be as little as an email address or a bigger commitment such as credit card details.

This commitment means that the Lead Generation Product is never truly 'free' but for a landing page to be effective, a customer's details need to be captured. In the 4 step lead generation process, we will refer to the term 'free' such as offering a free eBook but it's absolutely critical that basic contact information such as an email address is provided to make the process work.

Summary

Ultimately, it's up to you if you decide to limit the choices on your landing page or offer something for free but following the above guidelines will make a bigger impact on the results of your landing page. The main points in this chapter are:

That limiting choice - or ideally having no choice with just one single option! - will increase the number of people who decide to take the action you want them to.

Offering something for free is irresistible and should be used if the purpose of the landing page is to generate leads that result in a sale. Offering something that's free will increase the number of people who take action compared to asking for an immediate sale, although you must take action on the generated lead properly to drive them to an eventual sale (see chapter 4 about the 4 step lead generation process).

These two behaviors, especially the limiting of choice, also apply to websites in general. if you look at the home page of giants such as Twitter or Google search the options are limited. For Google, it's a clean page with a search box while on Twitter you have the choice to register or sign in with other options cleverly hidden away at the bottom of the page.

Now let's cover the 10 core elements of an effective landing page...

Chapter 3: 10 Core Elements Of An Effective Landing Page

So, what makes a highly effective landing page?

Here are the 10 core elements:

1. Clear Layout

White space is good!

Many marketers and business owners think it's important to load as much information as possible onto a page. After all, a busy page represents a busy, professional company, right? And people buy from businesses that are busy with customers that must trust them. Actually, this isn't strictly true. Having too much information crowded into a single page can have a negative impact.

The recommended number of words for a landing page is between 100 and 1,000 words. There is an argument (and evidence over the years from tests) that having more words rather than less can increase conversion rate as a customer spends more time finding out about what is on offer and buys into your brand over time.

However, with the rise in use of videos and shortening attention spans, people are reading less content and the number of words is becoming less relevant. It's important to grab the reader's attention as quickly as possible and to guide them towards taking the action you want. For this reason, what's important is the overall message on the page, how clearly it's communicated and other factors such as the call to action which will be discussed later.

Don't feel a need to fill a page with as much text as possible. Only include wording if it adds value and don't be afraid to have a good balance of white space (or whatever color background you decide to use on your site). The more distractions there are, the more diluted the key message and the prompt to take action will be.

Here are a few more points to think about when it comes to layout:

Try to avoid scrolling.

In a busy world where we are bombarded with information, it's incredible how quickly consumers can give up on a website when they come across the smallest of hurdles! It's proven that the more a visitor must click on links to other pages or scroll down a page the higher the bounce rate (and the lower the conversion rate).

In other words, for every click or scroll, the number of people staying on your site will go down. Imagine you have 100 people visit your site and need to click 3 times on a menu option to get what they want. It could be that as many as 10 or 15 will leave the site rather than click the first link. If 15 leave then out of the remaining 85 another, say 20 people will not click a second time, followed by another 20 who will not click a third time. The net result is that over half (or 55 out of 100) people have left the site because they don't have the patience to visit more web pages.

For many companies, a bounce rate of 70-80% is typical. This means that only 20 or 30 in every 100 are visiting a second page!

Use colors that get results

The colors you use on the landing page should always be in line with your overall branding but there's a little secret that not many people know – certain colors impact the way people think and the decisions they make!

According to Kissmetrics in their blog post (see link below), red "increases heart rate" and "creates urgency". Red is ideal as a call to action in discounted or clearance sales while orange is "aggressive" and "creates a call to action" such as "subscribe, buy or sell".

https://blog.kissmetrics.com/color-psychology/

Both red and orange are recommended for call to action buttons (see point 2 below for more information on call to actions) but if you want to increase trust in your landing page, consider blue.

If you sell luxury products, consider black as the main theme, while pink and purple are more effective with fashion and beauty products.

At the very least, ensure to use color and styling of the landing page in line with your branding and strongly consider orange or read for your call to action!

2. A Clear Call To Action With A Benefit

A landing page MUST have a call to action (CTA). It's the most important element of a landing page. Creating a landing page with no call to action is like a shop with no door for customers to come in or a car with no wheels. It might be a great looking car, but you won't be going anywhere with it!

If your web page tells people how great your service is and has lots of images but there is no way to make the purchase or find out more information, then customers will give up and go elsewhere.

The call to action must be clear and demonstrate the benefit of taking action. If, for example, you want people to sign up to your newsletter, then it should include why they should. Imagine you are looking for information and ideas on places to go on vacation or holiday. Which one of these two messages are you likely to act on?

Sign up for our newsletter!

Discover your next perfect holiday by email! Enter your email now.

The first one might suggest that lots of spammy emails are likely to arrive in my inbox soon, full of content that doesn't interest me. The last one, however, is much more appealing. I can see the benefit which is that I may discover my next perfect trip away.

It doesn't have to be to 'discover ideas for places to go'. It could be to save money with special offers or find out how to do something such as a hassle-free way to arrange your itinerary. Whatever the message is, it should be something that the reader sees the benefit of clicking on the link.

Using the right wording is important in the call to action as well as on the website in general. We will discuss the effective use of wording and the use of power words later in point 5, as it deserves a separate section for itself! In the meantime, here are some more important tips for designing your call to action:

Only Have One Call To Action (CTA)

It's tempting to make lots of different offers. Click here to get a discount coupon. Click here for a free guide. Click here to sign up to our newsletter. And click here to learn more in our weekly blog. The problem with all these call to actions is it will send different people in different directions and not where you want them to go.

I'm likely to navigate away from the landing page to read a blog post, never to return to the company's site again. You may be attracted to the newsletter or free guide and someone else may not be able to decide what they want to click on and they will visit a different site instead. All of this, when the company really wants visitors to click on the CTA to reveal the discount code and make a purchase!

Decide what you want your call to action to be and focus on that. You may decide that you want a second call to action if someone navigates away from the page, offering a special offer with a message such as:

Don't go just yet! How about an extra 10% off?

That's fine as it serves a different purpose with the assumption that the original call to action hasn't worked. In this example, you aren't presenting two CTAs at the same time. The second CTA only appears as the user navigates away and has decided the first CTA isn't relevant to them.

Make The Call To Action The Main Feature

A call to action should always stand out and always be very easily accessible. Whether a user reads the text on your page, watches a video or looks at the images he or she should always know where the call to action is and be attracted towards it.

If you are using video then it's recommended to mention the call to action at the end. Words or a voice saying 'click the button below to save money' or 'fill the form in now to get your free gift' will drive the website visitor back to the call to action.

Make It Simple To Take Action

I've heard discussions in marketing teams along the lines of "we should get as much data from the customer as possible so we should use a form requesting their name, age, address, what interests them..." but this isn't thinking about the customer. Why would anyone want to fill in all that information?

We have already discussed that people will abandon a website if they need to click and scroll too much and requesting excessive amounts of information has the same impact. In fact, the bounce rate is higher in this instance compared to scrolling or having extra clicks.

In eCommerce one of the biggest reasons for shopping cart abandonment is because consumers don't want to have to fill in so much information. I find it amazing that someone has browsed a shop, found what they want, clicked on the buy button and still not made the purchase because they can't be bothered to fill in their name and address, yet in their mind, they are 'bought in' to the idea of buying the product!

If visitors don't want to add information when buying something they like, why would they want to do it on a landing page for a free eBook or discount code?

If the purpose of the call to action is to add the site visitor to your email list for ongoing marketing campaigns, then just take their email address.

Adding their first name so that emails can be personal is a nice touch but always bear in mind that the more information you request, the fewer sign-ups you will get. You can always find out more about someone later once you have their initial details. You can't do that if they don't share anything at all.

If you absolutely must obtain some information, then you can always request basic information and when the visitor clicks on the submit button you can redirect them to another page requesting a bit more information.

This is a bit sneaky and possibly annoying if not done properly, but it will provide a higher sign-up rate than requesting all the information on the landing page. I suggest avoiding this unless you really have to.

Think About Timing With Pop-Ups

Having Pop-ups that appear on a page aren't the same as call to actions that are on a landing page but it's worth discussing them briefly at this point to understand how they can be used and how they compare to a call to action that is embedded into the page rather than popping up on the screen.

Pop-ups as the name suggests, suddenly appear or pop up while the user is on a website or web page. They are designed to stand out more as they appear on the screen rather than what you might consider blending into the text on a page.

The timing and position of a pop-up can vary and they are useful on pages that are not designed as a true landing page. The best option is to have it appear after the visitor has been on the site for a few seconds and to feature it prominently in the middle of the screen. Using Pop-ups as your main CTA has the disadvantage that they are not always on the page, so once a visitor closes the pop-up there is no longer a CTA.

The best method is to have a call to action that is on the page as a form or simple button (such as buy now) but if you must have a pop up on your landing page then consider where and when it pops up. A pop up that appears as soon as the visitor arrives on the page doesn't give the visitor time to find out any information about your product first. It is likely to alienate them and be perceived as being annoying.

The most effective pop-ups are those that either appear 10-20 seconds after arriving on the page or as the visitor moves the cursor to navigate away from the page as a backup secondary CTA.

Also, consider the following with pop-ups:

- Position the CTA in the middle of the screen or make it fullscreen
- Use the appropriate color and wording of the pop-up that's most effective
- Consider a pop-up that only appears once per visitor every 3 days or longer

Pop-ups are a great marketing tool that are effective if used properly, but if used badly, they serve only to annoy visitors who are slowly warming to your brand. If a visitor is coming back to your site, they might not want pop-ups to appear constantly and that's why most pop up apps now have the feature to limit how often a returning visitor sees them.

Test Your Call To Action

Call to actions are rarely perfect the first time and even if you have a strong call to action then there are still ways to make it perform better. It's recommended to test your CTA over time, making changes and then reviewing it to see if the conversion rate increases as a result of the changes you have made.

Before even posting your call to action you may want to pass it by friends or work colleagues to get their opinion. Present them with options and ask which call to action they are more likely to take action on.

At the very least, ask yourself, would I take action with this? Why would I? If you put yourself in your visitors' shoes and the CTA isn't compelling enough then it may need changing.

Also, make sure to read about the use of power words later in this book as they are important for a successful call to action!

** BONUS **

As a reader of this book, you are welcome to email me personally a call to action you have currently or are thinking of using and I will provide you with feedback and recommendations for FREE!

To get your Free CTA review, all you need to do is email me with your CTA or a link to it and the words 'FREE CTA REVIEW' and I will get back to you personally within 2-3 working days. To email me, use this address:

darren@thinktwicemarketing.com

Below are some examples of call to actions for different types of businesses. These are just examples and with a little bit of thought and trial, you may find they can be adapted and used for your own business!

Business Type	Call To Action
Business Coach	FREE Guide to delegating: How to delegate successfully so you can grow your business
Florist	£5 OFF: Enter your email address now to receive a coupon with £5 off your first order!
Technology Magazine	Stay ahead of the trend! Receive the latest news, trends, and technology tips by email
Estate Agent/Realtor	Be the first to find out about the latest hot properties for sale with our property updates. Sign up now!
Restaurant	Download our app with our latest offers and get 20% off your first meal. It's on us!
Hairdresser	Get great looking hairstyle ideas and offers with our weekly email. Sign up now!

The focus with all of these CTAs is on the value of taking the action. Each CTA gives a reason for taking the action which should be of value to the target audience.

A business coach, for example, is better offering something that he can help a client with such as improving productivity and better delegation rather than something generic like a free Amazon voucher or promotional material that people who are not his or her target audience might be interested in.

With a shopping voucher, it's possible to get a lot of people signing up to get the voucher when they have no interest in your service at all. But, they wouldn't download something relevant such as how to delegate within teams unless it was of use to them. This makes prospects much more relevant.

3. Use Video To Tell A Story

For many reasons (outlined in chapter 1), the world is moving towards more visual content. If you lead a busy life and suffer information overload then watching a short video is much more appealing than reading a load of text. Likewise, adding a video allows you to stand out compared to your competitors' landing pages.

Adding a video to your landing page allows visitors to hear and see what you offer. While extra effort is required to read words, a video is more stimulating and information such as product benefits are easier to absorb. That's why website landing pages with video are proven to convert at a higher rate.

If possible, try to tell a story with video (and I don't mean some long-winded sleepy bedtime stories that will turn readers away!). Use story-style content to help your audience understand what your offer or service can do for them.

If your service solves a specific problem, explain how if they click on the call to action then those problems will be solved. If you have an example of a customer experience you would like to share, then use this to add strength to your reasoning!

With attention spans shortening and more people reading on mobile phones, video is perfect for a landing page. If you are unsure how to go about creating an effective video, get in touch. We work with several partners who are professionals in effective video design.

You may alternatively want to check out screen recording tools such as Jing, Screencastify or Loom (https://www.loom.com)

There are also various tools such as or Animoto (https://animoto.com), Adobe Spark or Raw Shorts (www.rawshorts.com) which allow you to create animated short videos that are perfect for a landing page.

There have been various sources showing how much higher engagement and conversion rates are when using video and while the numbers vary, they are still big.

In 2017, Wordstream reported (amongst other data) that:

51% of marketing professionals worldwide name video as the type of content with the best ROI

Marketers who use video grow revenue 49% faster than non-video users.

Sixty-four percent of consumers make a purchase after watching branded social videos

Video on a landing page can increase conversions by 80% or more

According to Optinmonster (2019), 'video marketers get 66% more qualified leads per year'

It's possible to make good videos nowadays at a very low cost. It just requires a bit of thought (sometimes a lot of patience!) and some creativity!

4. Create Urgency Or Scarcity

In his book, *Oversubscribed*, Daniel Priestley gives examples of how companies have successfully generated sales by offering an element of uniqueness or exclusivity to customers. If a product is unique, in scarce supply or an offer is about to run out then the desire to take action is greater.

Take the following example:

FREE eBook on how to double your sales on eBay. Click here to grab your copy:

Free eBook on how to double your sales on eBay. Offer ends in 2 hours. Grab your copy now before it's too late!

If this offer is of interest, you are more likely to be prompted by the last message showing urgency. If the offer ends in 12 months or never at all then the human brain is likely to think along the lines of: 'that sounds interesting but I have got other stuff to do. I'll get the offer later when I have time' and guess what? As the days go by, you forget the offer and are still busy (aren't we always?). The opportunity is gone and the visitor is lost, most likely forever. An offer that finishes very soon means that the reader is at risk of missing out and they are more likely to take action.

Airlines are very good at taking advantage of the fear of scarcity. Ever looked at booking a flight only to see the message '2 seats left'? Websites for booking hotels are the same and Amazon also has a stock status which helps encourage shoppers to place the order before it's too late.

There are only so many places on a plane (or at a training session for example) and a short message that either says how many spaces are left or when the offer expires is enough to create urgency and prompt the visitor to take advantage – and not lose out!

Note: When we talk about creating urgency or scarcity, make sure to use it ethically. Telling people there are only 2 seats left at your event when there are a lot more is not just unethical, it's bad marketing in the long term and could prove embarrassing if you get found out.

I was recently on a webinar by a company called Teachable who offer a hosting platform for providing training courses and they were suggesting from research that training courses which have a short timeframe to enroll on are much more successful in signing up students than courses which are available to enroll for any time throughout the year. This makes sense and is in line with everything that I have said so far. If you want to create an offer that you use regularly but aren't sure how to use the scarcity factor then consider having several periods throughout the year when the offer is available.

Doing it this way allows you to generate some excitement and urgency and still be able to run the promotion over a longer period of time.

5. Use Power Words

Using Power words is one of my favorite topics when it comes to marketing and for good reason! So many people under-appreciate the power of using the right words and with a few changes to their wording, they could get much better results from marketing campaigns (including websites, social media posts, email marketing and so on).

According to Buffer in their blog article '189 Powerful Words That Convert' (available at blog.bufferapp.com/words-and-phrases-that-convert-ultimate-list), power words are so important that in a marketing campaign 'one word can change everything'. I completely agree. Adding one single power word could increase conversions on your landing page by as much as 20%.

Power words are, as the name suggests, words that hold power. They make a difference and have a higher impact when making a statement. Would you be more inclined to take action if someone tells you their services will **guarantee** results rather than just tells you they will get results? Would you rather I helped you to create a marketing campaign or to create a **successful** marketing campaign?

The word 'successful' is suggestive and makes the offer more desirable while 'guarantee' reduces the risk of buying the services and increases the confidence in what is being bought.

Sometimes a power word can be a simple adjective (or word that describes something) that is positive in nature. A restaurant may offer **delicious** ice cream while a team building events company may offer 5 **incredible** ways to motivate team members.

Many power words aren't descriptive but can be even more powerful. The word 'now' and 'hurry' are examples.

During our childhood, we are trained to do things 'now'. Screaming parents to the tune of 'put your shoes on now', 'we are running late, eat your food now' and 'for the fifth time, brush your teeth now!' may be great examples, some of us may remember well!

Upon reading the word 'now' many visitors are prompted at a subconscious level to take action. Who would have thought three letters could be so powerful!

Similarly, the word 'hurry' as in the sentence 'hurry, this offer won't last!' is claimed to prompt the reader to take action. It tells the user's brain at a subconscious level to hurry into action and click on the buy button (although it is effective from feedback, I don't believe it's quite as effective as the word 'now' which invokes a much stronger response).

I won't list a whole heap of power words here but you can access a larger list in my blog post 'Over 100 Power Words To Help You Convert More Customers' which is available at:

http://blog.quotini.co.uk/2017/01/over-100-power-words-to-help-you.html

Here are 30 power words worth considering that are particularly useful for a landing page:

Achieve – Amazing – Authentic – Avoid

Best-Selling – Easily – Exclusive – Free

Guarantee(d) – Hurry – Improved – Instantly

Jaw-dropping – Limited - No-Risk – Now

Offer – Only – Priceless – Quick – Proven

Remarkable – Results – Safe – Secret

Successful – Tested – You – Unique - Value

When writing copy for your landing page, make sure to use power words. It's also strongly recommended to review the wording before posting it to see where power words can be added. Read what you have written and ask at every point – can I add a power word in here that will make a difference to a visitor taking action? Obviously, don't go overkill by sticking power words everywhere. It's important to find the right balance and keep the content easy to read and for the message to be clearly understood.

Visitors may be put off by your 'incredible, unique, amazing limited time offer for your proven product that you must take advantage of now and that is exclusive and only available to you...'. Yawn.

6. Demonstrate Social Proof

The world has gone review mad! Want to buy a fridge? Check out the reviews before buying. Want to book a holiday? Check out the reviews on the location you fancy going to. Looking for somewhere fancy to take your partner to wine and dine? Check out what comes up in the top reviews.

Reviews have become a powerful part of the decision-making process for almost anything nowadays and for good reason. There are plenty of untrustworthy builders and online scammers that are quick to take your money and then run away with it. Reviews keep businesses focused on delivering great products and a high level of customer service.

Ask a genuinely good builder and he or she will tell you how unethical competitors and scammers have given their industry a bad reputation. Having genuine reviews makes a huge difference as it helps provide a high level of trust in the services you offer. Having a customer say you are fantastic holds a lot more power with another customer than you saying how good you are.

Social proof can come in many forms such as showing how long you have been established, that you are a human caring business through social media or by demonstrating testimonials and reviews on your website.

Providing social proof on a landing page can take a customer's final decision from 'I'm not sure enough if I want to buy' to 'ok, let's do this. I will make the purchase'.

The type of social proof you use can vary depending, firstly on what social proof you already have and secondly on what you believe is more likely to convert visitors for your particular offering or industry.

Here are some examples of social proof you can include:

- Downloads: Over 10,000 people have downloaded already!
- Growing social presence: Join the 1,000 people who have liked us already!
- Purchasing: A customer testimonial such as "Great product. Anyone would be crazy to miss out on having this!"
- Booking a restaurant or hotel: Over 500 people have rated us 5 stars!
- Booking a hotel: We have won the TripAdvisor and Late Rooms award for the best quality service in 2019!
- Membership: Over 1,000 people have joined our community already!

One thing to avoid with adding social proof is directing visitors away from the landing page. You may have a separate page full of reviews but redirecting them away from the landing page increases the risk that they will not click on the call to action on the landing page that you want them to.

Remember in point 2 above, we talked about only having one single call to action and avoiding having other links. We have also briefly mentioned having testimonials from customers in a video. Having the voice of a customer saying 'these services changed my life' or 'these products are incredible, my business is more profitable as a result' is much more credible than you saying this or simply putting their words into quotes.

SSL Certification

This topic is something that could almost have its own section on as it's so important! However, it's not something that we need to cover in detail. If you aren't familiar with SSL certification, it's the difference between your website starting with http or https. The added 's' stands for secure and if your website isn't secure then the internet browser your visitor is using to visit your site may come up with a message such as 'this website is not secure' followed by something like 'your personal details may be at risk if you visit this site'. I have also seen instances where visiting the site is blocked and the Chrome browser warns strongly not to proceed to the site.

When it comes to generating leads and giving social proof that your brand is worthy, the last thing you want is your visitors being told that your site isn't safe!

If your website starts http:// (without the S) then you need to make it secure and converted to https. The process for having SSL certification varies depending on what hosting platform you are using and how you registered your website address. The technicalities of sorting this out aren't covered here but you may need to talk to your web designer. Platforms such as weebly allow you to turn your site into a secure one by ticking a box in the settings.

7. Make It Personal

This principle applies to many types of marketing campaigns such as email and social media marketing. The more personal you make your landing page, the more a visitor is likely to relate to the offer and be inclined to take action.

According to 'Yes!: 50 Secrets From the Science of Persuasion' by Noah Goldstein, there is evidence that a customer is more likely to buy from a salesperson with the same name! People respond to surveys more if it's provided by someone with a similar name and evidence exists that people tend to choose careers that are similar to them in name (such as Denise working at a dentist or George working in the specialty of Geography!).

Subconsciously we can relate to these similarities such as our name as they are personal to us. Personality increases familiarity and if a potential customer becomes more familiar with your brand then this increases the chances of a purchase.

In email marketing, it's much easier to send emails with the recipient's name in, but with landing pages it's not so easy. It is, however, still possible to make the page as personal as possible.

If you know your target audience has particular tastes or likes, then consider using that to your advantage and focus on using the tone and wording in the message that your audience speaks.

The tone and wording should still always be in line with the tone of your brand whilst making it personal. If your website is serious and professional in style, it might seem odd if you create a landing page that is the opposite. A bright, funky looking site in this instance risks putting customers off. Similarity builds trust!

The easiest way to make a landing personal is to refer to situations in the second person rather than third. Instead of words like 'they' and 'people' use 'you' and 'your'. These are power words that people are more comfortable with as they feel you are talking to them directly.

Instead of saying 'grab a copy' or 'download a copy', say 'grab your copy'. Instead of saying 'this product improves productivity' say 'improve your productivity' or 'be more productive in what you do'.

If your business offering involves human interactions then having a picture of you or the team that will be involved in the experience also adds a personal touch. Similarly, a video with you included will help the website visitor relate to you and your business better. And the more they can relate on a personal level, the more likely they are to buy.

8. Good Quality Images

For many website visitors, if there is any doubt about the quality or legitimacy of what you offer and who you are then they will quickly walk away - and the quality of images on your landing page will play their part.

Poor quality images can put a visitor off and cast doubt on the overall brand but great images, well placed can make a huge difference. After all, a picture says a thousand words!

Using your own images is much better than using stock images and if you aren't very good at taking photos, there are plenty of online tools that you can use to improve the quality of images you have taken. You can also take stock images from sites such as Pixabay and Pexels and use them as part of a custom image that you can create yourself using an app such as Canva, RelayThat or Stencil. Doing it this way means you can create stunning images for a relatively low-cost and what you produce doesn't look like stock images.

Most apps also have templates that you can use that look good and can save you time.

Here are some general tips on images to consider:

- Images of people (or cats and dogs) work better than static objects
- Use images that reflect the outcome or experience of your service
- Avoid stock images where possible
- Use images that relate to what the site says or the overall message
- Don't overcrowd the page with images
- Avoid poor quality images at all cost!

If you experience the latter point then you can use sites such as www.fiverr.com and www.peopleperhour.com and pay a relatively low cost for someone to smarten up your image or even create something for you. You can also create your own visual content using Canva (visit www.canva.com).

If you are using video on your landing page, then it's most likely that fewer images are needed. Remember to always keep the layout simple and clean.

9. Get The Right Benefits Across

The benefits of what you are offering must be clear. As a rule, try to include your one key benefit in your call to action and get across the 3-4 main benefits on the landing page. This number may vary slightly depending on what you offer but always try to limit how many benefits you feature. Otherwise, you risk having a confusing message.

If you aren't sure what your one key benefit is, write the benefits down on a piece of paper then compare them to see what you or your customers believe is the most important. Here's an example:

A business app that is designed to track meetings and what's discussed as well as the agreed actions are might have the following benefits:

- More effective meetings
- Keep the team informed on meeting topics and actions
- Hold attendees accountable to their actions
- Improve collaboration and teamwork
- Save time: reduced the number of hours spent by having fewer meetings
- Free up resources that could be used on other activities
- Never miss a project deadline
- … and so on.

Out of these benefits, the company offering the app may decide that the one key benefit is how much time is saved using the app. In this case, the CTA might be 'Save time with more effective meetings download the app now!'.

3-4 additional benefits could be listed on the landing page such as:

- Improve collaboration and teamwork
- Free up resources that could be used on other activities
- Never miss a project deadline

Listing any more benefits on a single page without scrolling or being distracted should be enough to get the message across. If you are using video, these key benefits should be included.

Note: You may disagree with the benefits I have chosen in the above example. This is just an example of how the benefits should be shortlisted and the point here is to get across enough key benefits concisely - and in a way that the reader will understand why they should buy. If you list lots of benefits, the reader is likely to get bored or information overload and navigate away to something more attention-grabbing.

10. Implement, Review, Change and Test again

All landing pages should be reviewed continuously and modified where appropriate to make them more effective. Note that I say 'continuously' as it's not just a one-off review. By regularly evaluating the page and trying different things you can really make a landing page highly tuned up to get results.

We will now discuss the process of Implement, Review, Change and Test again in more detail.

Implement

You never know how well a landing page is going to work until it's published and marketed. It's at this point that you may start to discover that what you believed was a great call to action or page structure isn't as good as you thought it was.

Feedback before launching maybe that it looks good but in reality, it isn't converting. It's always easy for people to say a page looks nice but that doesn't mean they will buy from it (as discussed early on in this book!).

Even if your page is converting well, can you convert better? Unless you are converting every single visitor then the likelihood is that you can get better results!

Review

Before publishing your page, make sure you are using Google Analytics or a similar tool. Google Analytics allows you to track how many unique and returning visitors there are to your landing page. From this you can then calculate your conversion rate using the following formula:

Conversion rate (%) = sign-ups to your call to action/total visitors

Sign-ups to your call to action is the number of people who have clicked on the CTA and completed the action. If your call to action is to sign up for a newsletter, then it will be the number of people who have signed up for your newsletter.

If your call to action is to download a free guide, then it will be the number of people who have clicked the call to action to get their free guide.

Imagine that in January you had 1,000 visits to your landing page and 50 people signed up for your newsletter. This means your conversion rate is 5%. The calculation would be:

Conversion rate = 50/1000 or 5%

Why Total Visitors and not unique visitors?

Google Analytics displays data for unique visitors and returning visitors. Together these make up the total visitors to your site or webpage.

My preference is to use total visitors and base the calculations on the number of visits to the site in total. The reason for this is that the term 'unique visitors' is misleading.

If I visit your web page several times, I might look at it on my desktop at home, laptop at work and then on my mobile. Because I have looked at the page using different connection types, in three different geographic locations, Google is likely to count that as three unique visits when in fact it's only one. Google does take measures to reduce the chances of your visits counting as multiple users but it's not foolproof.

The measurement of unique visitors isn't the number of unique people, it's based on unique access locations or cookies. Comparing unique visitors to your site to returning visitors is a great way to understand your target audience and website visitors but I don't recommend using unique visitors in the above formula.

According to data from 2014*, the average conversion rate across industries is 2.74%. A conversion rate of 5-10% is considered very good and how high or low your conversion rate is should help determine how much change you need to make to your landing page content and design. A conversion rate of below 2% raises means there is considerable scope for improvement whereas if you have a conversion rate of 5% or higher then it's best to be more cautious in the changes you make. The last thing you want to do is make changes to your landing page and find your conversion rate has plummeted!

When reviewing the results, ask the following questions:

- Are the right people arriving on my site? (If not, review the activities you use to drive visitors to your page)
- Are the benefits and the key message clear and compelling enough?

- What elements exist on the page that put doubt into the minds of the visitor? (it could be that it lacks social proof or looks too unprofessional or 'cheesy' in style)
- Is the call to action too difficult to access or not standing out enough?
- If most visitors are using mobile (according to Google Analytics), is my site optimised for this?
- Does the page have distractions that are driving visitors away from the CTA?

On the last point, you can check this out by viewing the User Flow in Google Analytics. If you have links to other pages on your site, then you will be able to see how many visitors are visiting other pages from your landing page.

Heatmaps are also a good way to understand what visitors are doing on your page. There are a number of apps (see suggested tools below) which can be installed on your landing page and show mouse movements and clicks on your site.

As a reader of my book, you are welcome to contact me personally for a free 15-minute review of your landing page results. I also offer a full more detailed review including an analysis of website visits using Google Analytic (providing you have this set up!). Get in touch to find out more.

Change and Test Again

When making changes to your site, try not to make too many changes at once. Often and frequent changes are better as you can review the results of each change. For example, you may have a conversion rate of 1%. You make a small change of moving the call to action higher up the screen and 2 weeks later, you see your conversion rate has jumped to 3%. You know from this that it has worked, but if you have made multiple changes you won't know what has worked – and what hasn't!

We have now covered the 10 core elements to a successful landing page. Here is a summary of the 10 elements we have discussed:

1. Have a landing page with a clear layout

2. Use a clear Call To Action (CTA) with a benefit

3. Use video to tell a story

4. Create urgency or scarcity

5. Use Power Words

6. Demonstrate social proof

7. Make it personal

8. Use good quality images

9. Get the right benefits across

10. Implement, review, change and test again

Using these elements you will be able to create a highly effective landing page that people will take action on.

Examples of good and bad landing pages

Below is the link to a short video I have done showing examples of well designed landing pages. Make sure to use the link below as you won't find this video publicly on YouTube! It's restricted to make it exclusive to purchasers of this and my other books.

I recommend watching the video as it will help to understand and visually see the elements of design that work:

https://youtu.be/UToDOAgqMW4

Below is another link with some brief examples of landing pages and call to actions that are ineffective:

https://youtu.be/Tg-IPzrjS58

In the next chapter, I will go through the proven four-step lead generation process which a well designed landing page must be part of.

Chapter 4: The Four-Step Lead Generation Process

We have already mentioned that a landing page can be used in many ways to grow sales and one method I use for myself and my customers is what I call my proven four-step lead generation process. This process involves using a landing page as one of four key ingredients.

The use of this process can apply to anyone selling to business customers as well as consumers and can even be used for eCommerce businesses. The process uses four key ingredients:

The promotional trigger
The landing page
The Lead Generation Product
The email marketing campaign

The **promotional trigger** is used to reach out to your target audience and drive them to your landing page. It will include a call to action, offering your Lead Generation Product.

A **Lead Generation Product** is a product that is not your core product. It is something that is offered to customers as part of the sales process and that requires a potential customer to give away some details, typically an email address in exchange for the product. This information is then used as part of the lead generation and conversion process.

The promotional trigger could be a Facebook Ads campaign offering a free eBook (as the **Lead Generation Product**). When the advert is clicked it will take the prospect to the **landing page** where they enter their email address in exchange for the eBook. Once this is done, an automated **email marketing campaign** starts with an initial email including the link to the eBook.

The email marketing campaign will then move the prospect towards making a purchase of the core products and services that you sell. I mentioned 'automated' as the move effective lead generation process will involve a series of automated emails but this can be done manually. Doing it manually has disadvantages such as the amount of time needed to follow up on a large number of leads and the risk of mistakes and delays in sending out emails if staff are away or it's the weekend.

Using a personal fitness trainer as an example, the process and key ingredients would look something like this:

The promotional trigger:
A Facebook Ads campaign offering a free guide to healthy eating. Targeting people on Facebook who live nearby and have expressed an interest in fitness.

The landing page:
Purely focused on getting the visitor to enter their email address to receive their free guide.

The Lead Generation Product:
The free guide is delivered via email once the customer has entered their email address

The email marketing campaign:
Starts with an email containing the link to the free guide followed by a series of emails providing top tips on getting fit and eating well. The emails will contain offers such as a free initial chat with the personal trainer or coupons to get 4 sessions for the price of 3.

It's important during the email marketing to offer valuable and relevant content. This will keep them subscribed and warmed up to the idea of receiving your emails that they want to read. The offers should vary since everyone is different and one particular offer is not going to be for everybody. The 4 sessions for the price of 3 might be a bit too much for some people but a free initial chat or 20% off your first session might be perfect for them.

The four-step lead generation process is proven to get results and the details of the different ingredients will vary depending on the type of business you are in. The promotional trigger could, for example, be a Google Adwords campaign for people searching for what you offer or it could be a LinkedIn Ads campaign to business owners.

The whole process is focused around finding a new customer, reaching out to them and capturing their email address so that you can continue to market to them in a way that generates sales.

The Lead Generation Product that you offer MUST be strongly related to what you offer in your business. There is no point offering something like free Amazon vouchers as this will generate interest from people who are not interested in your product or service.

If you are a florist, offer a guide on buying or looking after flowers. If you are an estate agent or realtor then offer a guide to buying the right house. I wouldn't download a guide to buying flowers or houses unless I had an active interest in buying flowers or a house.

Done this way, you know that the emails you receive are at least from prospects who have an interest in what you offer. Someone who does have an interest in flowers or buying a property is highly like to provide their email address in exchange for some valuable tips to help them with their purchase.

Now we have covered the important elements of a landing page and how it can be part of the four step lead generation process let's discuss the process for handing prospects who have taken action on the site in more detail.

Chapter 5: Life After The Landing Page

Post-Landing Page Automation

Once a visitor acts on your landing page, some form of activity is required. If the call to action is to buy from an eCommerce site or redirect the visitor to a new page to access information, then this can easily be set up when creating the landing page but other actions may need extra design and implementation.

If your objective is to offer a free guide or eBook in exchange for an email address that you want to use as part of an email marketing campaign then a more complex solution is needed. You could manage this manually but as I have mentioned earlier, this is a huge waste of time and risks errors, such as forgetting to send the right email at the right time (especially if you are out of the office for a few days or more!).

Here are some top tips and ideas for automating the process:

How To Automate Offering Your Free Service

There are several ways you can do this. You could redirect the visitor to a page on your site where they can download it. You could email them a link to where it's stored either on your website or in a shared location such as Google Drive or Dropbox.

Or you could deliver the 'download' as text in an email. In this case, it's not really a download so the offer would need to be worded differently to say that the visitor can access top tips or a free guide rather than download it.

The most effective option is to redirect the visitor to a page where it can be downloaded AND to follow up immediately with an email containing the link to that page. This means the visitor has immediate access to the document and gets used to receiving emails from you.

It also has the added benefit that the visitor can access the document at any time using the email in their inbox!

An Example Setup Of An Automated Process

Tools for email marketing and making your freebie available are listed below (See Tools To Help You Create The Perfect Landing Page) but for now, I'm going to refer to two tools that I particularly like: SumoMe and MailChimp. This is just an example, but many tools like SumoMe and MailChimp integrate together to perform a similar function.

SumoMe is available as a plugin for WordPress allowing you to present a call to action on your site and capture an email address. It integrates with (amongst others) MailChimp which can be used to store the email addresses you capture and send out emails.

Here is how an automated process might be set up using these tools:

- SumoMe is used to provide a call to action and capture an email address
- When the CTA is clicked, the visitor is redirected to a download page
- AND SumoMe sends the email address entered to list automatically in your MailChimp account
- MailChimp automatically sends out a thank you email including the link to the new email address that has been added
- A series of emails are sent out automatically by MailChimp over several weeks with information, tips and offers to the subscriber
- Over time the potential customer will act on one of your call to actions (most likely from your email marketing) and purchase from you

This may sound complex and it does require a bit of work initially but once it's set up, the whole process runs automatically. This is just one example of how two tools can be used with a landing page as part of a very effective long term marketing campaign to capture leads and convert customers from visitors to customers. See below for more tools to consider.

If you are serious about creating a marketing process that works using a landing page and automated email marketing then you may be interested in my book 'How To Create A Successful Email Marketing Campaign', available on Amazon. In this book, I cover the benefits of using email marketing and a landing page to convert customers as well as information on how to set up the process and create emails that convert customers from the landing page.

To purchase this book, visit Amazon and search by my name: **Darren Hignett** or by the book title: ***How To Create A Successful Email Marketing Campaign***.

Manual Follow Up

The simplest way to follow up is a manual email but there are a number of limitations such as the amount of work involved (it's manual!) and the fact that the potential customer might not yet be ready to buy. Another way to follow up manually and be more efficient is to follow up when the customer is more likely to buy.

Using an email marketing client, you can segment and extract prospects that are more likely to purchase. For example, a prospect that downloads your free guide opens 2 or more out of 5 emails and clicks on links within those emails clearly has an interest in the type of services you offer.

At this stage, it's time to send a personal follow up email or make a phone call to generate the sale. If you don't like cold calling, don't worry. It isn't. The prospect is certainly warmed up to you by this stage so rest assured it's more like a 'warm' or 'hot call'!

By using this kind of filtering, you can reduce time wasted on contacting people who are not interested. If you receive 100 signups a day, that's a lot of phone calls or follow-ups to do but if only 30 people meet the above criteria then you know they are more likely to buy from you than the other 70.

The limits you set are up to you and will vary depending on what you offer and other factors such as how many emails you send out. Choose a threshold and a follow up activity that you feel comfortable with. You can always change it later.

Converting None-Converters

Ideally, you want to focus on people who have signed up or taken action on your site. At this stage, you are probably thinking 'well, I can't do anything about people who don't provide details anyway' but actually, it is possible.

Tools exist (see tools below) which allow you to identify anonymous visitors to your site. Once installed on your landing page you will be able to see the name and details of a company that has visited your site. They cost money but can provide a great return if you take action by contacting these companies to see how you can help.

If you are getting many visitors, then you can select the visitors that have the largest potential.

Chapter 6: Promoting Your Landing Page

So far we have discussed how to create a landing page that either converts a web visitor into a paying customer or captures their email address and other contact information. We have also discussed post landing page activities (in other words, what you do with that contact information to convert them into a paying customer) but we haven't discussed how to get prospects to your landing page!

The best landing page and email marketing campaign to visitors of the page is wasted if no one visits your page! There are many ways to drive visitors to your site which we will discuss now.

Here are some examples of ways you can attract your target audience to your landing page:

Social Media posts and Advertising

At the very least you should schedule content regularly to tell people about what you are offering on your landing page. Posts such as 'Learn how to be more productive' or 'Discover great ways to eat healthily with this free eBook! Click here to find out more:' will encourage your followers to visit your landing page.

You can also write content in a more personal way such as 'I've just launched my new landing page offering a free eBook on healthy eating. Take a look and let me know what you think!'. Assuming that people are following you on social media because they have an interest in what you do, some followers will at least visit your page to find out more.

Unfortunately, just posing to existing fans has limitations. Some may already be customers and even if they aren't, your posts are limited to your existing number of fans and anyone else who finds your posts on social media. Social media posting is free but limited and needs to be combined with paid advertising, even if you only spend a small amount.

Advertising on social media is a great way to reach many more people in a very short period of time. At Think Twice Marketing, we often tell customers that efforts put into social media marketing will not be as effective as it should be if paid advertising isn't used. There is a cost involved but this should outweigh the number of leads you can generate as a result of running an advertising campaign.

Just spending a few dollars or pounds to boost a post on Facebook means that hundreds, possibly thousands of people will see your Ad.

We won't go through the different social platforms and advantages of advertising on each one here (that's either for a new book and is included in our Social Media For Business Results course available online). But we will discuss Facebook and LinkedIn.

For most businesses, Facebook is highly effective as it's relatively cheap and their target audience can be reached. I often hear people say their target audience isn't on Facebook but with over 2 billion users worldwide, it's hard to believe that anyone selling Business to Business (B2B) can't find business owners, sales managers or other people with similar job titles personally using Facebook.

With Facebook, you can either boost a post you have created about your landing page offer (the easiest option) or create an Ad using the Facebook Ads manager (the harder but more effective option). Either way, you will need to set up a Facebook Ads account when you are logged in to Facebook.

If you are planning to use Facebook Ads seriously and spend money regularly promoting your offer then I strongly recommend creating a proper Ad. From my own experience and feedback from other sources including marketing experts, there are too many limitations when boosting a post and Facebook seems to charge more money for less results. Boosting a post should be kept to occasional use to support a full Facebook Ads campaign.

LinkedIn is especially powerful for business to business as you can accurately target people based on job roles and industries. If you are targeting sales managers in the Paris area for software companies with more than 10 employees then you can. Facebook doesn't have that level of targeting for B2B but is much cheaper than LinkedIn Ads.

With LinkedIn Ads, you can also send a promotional message to someone's inbox. This is highly effective as people respond more to personal messages than an Ad they see at the top of a browser or in their newsfeed.

Search Ads

Google Ads is a great way to target people who are actively searching for what you offer. A wedding planner offering a free guide to planning a wedding can create an ad for people who search for keywords such as 'wedding planner guide' or 'wedding checklist'. Someone offering admin services to businesses could offer their free guide to being more productive when people search for 'productivity tips' or 'how to prioritise work tasks'.

In the title, I say 'Search Ads' but have so far talked about Google. There are other options such as Bing Search from Microsoft but Google is so dominant in the worldwide market that the first place to start with is Google. Having said that, Bing is still worth considering as there are less people competing to promote their business but this has to be balanced against the smaller target audience you will reach.

Whether it's advertising on social media or through Google, make sure to set your budget and evaluate the results before you spend any more. If the cost per click (how much it costs every time someone clicks on your Ad) is too high and your margins are already low then it can easily eat away at your margin.

A campaign might cost $2 per click but if it takes 10 or 20 clicks for every sale then that's an extra $20-$40 cost for every sale you make. This might be ok for you but it's important to monitor your spend and ROI.

If you need help setting up an Ads campaign on Google or a social media platform such as Facebook then get in touch. I'm happy to discuss how I can help.

Other online channels

There are many other ways to promote your landing page online. Here's a list of ideas:

Trade and industry websites as advertising

Posting in relevant LinkedIn and Facebook Groups

Sharing links on forums including Quora and Reddit

Emailing your existing database of contacts about the new landing page

Optimizing your landing page to appear in Google Search results

Create a blog post about the offer and promote it through various channels

Offline activities

There are also various offline ways to promote your landing page such as advertising in a trade or business magazine that is purchased (or is available for free) for your target audience. Many businesses are now finding promotional materials sent by post are effective as there is much less competition compared to advertising online.

Offline and online can also be combined. Telling a publication or PR agency, for example, about what you offer could lead to promoting your landing page in a printed publication as well as on their website.

Above are just a few ways to promote your landing page. The important takeaway is that you must promote your landing page! Having a well designed landing page is great but ineffective if nobody is visiting it!

The next chapter discusses some tools that you can use to create an effective landing page. Don't forget to check out the bonus offers at the end including some extra free materials, available only to you as a purchaser of this book!

Chapter 7: Tools to Help You Create The Perfect Landing Page

There are many tools available to help you create the perfect landing page, whether it's assistance with image design, pop up call to actions or email marketing.

I have separated the different apps and tools into different categories to make it clearer and added comments where appropriate.

(Note: Some of these require a paid subscription).

Creating Landing Pages

WordPress

Weebly (and other sites such as WIX)

ClickFunnels

Adpage (https://adpage.io/en/)

Adpage is designed specifically for creating landing pages rather than full-blown branded websites. It has a range of templates to choose from as well as features such as a countdown timer that you can add to your landing pages.

Storing and Sharing Freebies

Google Drive

Dropbox

OneDrive

Creating Forms

SumoMe

WuFoo

JotForm

Form Stack

123 Contact Form

Cognito Form

Creating Pop-ups

Wise Pops (www.wisepops.com)

SumoMe

Scroll Trigger Boxes for WordPress (www.wordpress.org/plugins/scroll-triggered-boxes)

Other WordPress plugins include: Hello Bar, Mango Buttons, WordPress Calls To Action and WP Pop Up

Email Marketing Software

MailChimp

Constant Contact

Campaign Monitor

AWeber

Vertical Response

Other email software solutions include: Emma (www.myemma.com), Mad Mimi, FeedBlitz, Inbox First, Klaviyo, Vero, Drip, MailerLite, WhatCounts, ConvertKit

Tools For Tracking Anonymous Site Visitors

Lead Forensics

Ruler Analytics (www.ruleranalytics.com)

Lead Feeder

Who Is Visiting (www.whoisvisiting.com)

Image Design

Canva

Stencil (www.getstencil.com)

RelayThat

Automated Integration Tools

These tools can be used to integrate two or more apps. They act as a bridge between them.

Zapier

IFTTT

Tracking Visitor On-Page Movement (heatmaps)

SumoMe Heat Maps Pro App

Navilytics (includes other clever page analysis features!)

Creating A Free Guide Or EBook

Beacon (www.beacon.by)

Blurb

eBook Adaptations

Creating Low Cost Video With Screen Capture

Screencastify (Google Chrome extension)

Jing

Loom

Creating Animated Videos

Raw Shorts

Animoto

Fully functioning powerful software solutions

Hubspot

Wishpond (focused specifically on landing page automation)

Kissmetrics

Infusionsoft

Ontraport

GetResponse

Pardot

Bonus Offers

I'm really delighted that you have chosen to read my book and am always keen to make sure readers get the best value out of my books as possible. Below are some offers, only offered through my books:

Free mini eBook on Email Marketing

This mini eBook covers some basic terminologies of email marketing along with some ideas for using email marketing effectively.

Free landing page checklist

What we have covered in this book is summed up in this checklist with a list of activities to do and things that you must check that you don't have!

To grab a copy of one or both of these, email me directly using my email address shown below and indicating which offers you would like. In order to keep these offers exclusive they are not available on any website. If you email me you won't be added to any marketing list and you will get a personal email back from me.

Email: darren@thinktwicemarketing.com

How about a review?

Now you have read this book, I'm sure you will appreciate how important it is to have social proof and having a positive review is one great way to show this. The challenge I hear from business owners - and that I experience as well, is getting even the most delighted customers to leave a testimonial! If you have enjoyed this book and found it useful then I would love to have a review.

Leaving a review for this book helps others by showing them what you think. I would really love it if you did and I'm offering a month of two months free access to the Ultimate Digital Marketing course which is available online. To get this, simply leave a review and email me a link to the review using the above email address. I will come back to you with full details and a coupon you can use, granting 2 months free access.

Thanks, And Good Luck!

In this book, we have covered what makes a highly effective landing page including tools that can be used to help with the appearance of the landing page and the sales process, including after the landing page has been visited by a potential customer.

I hope this short concise book has been of use to you. I highly recommend referring back to it during the creation of any new landing page as well as when reviewing the performance of existing pages on your site. If you have any questions, don't hesitate to get in touch with me via email. My email address is below.

Thanks for reading and good luck with your website marketing!

Darren

Email Address: darren@thinktwicemarketing.com

For more books by me, visit my UK Amazon Profile:

My .com profile:

https://www.amazon.com/Darren-Hignett/e/B00Q08P95M

My UK (.co.uk) profile:

https://www.amazon.co.uk/Darren-Hignett/e/B00Q08P95M

PS. **Don't forget to help others by leaving a review!**

Made in the USA
Columbia, SC
01 February 2021